This Journal Belongs To:

_____

Practicing gratitude has proven benefits to not only improve our mental health but our relationship with our self and others. Start experiencing more joy and happiness today by using this book for your daily gratitude practice!

Some Tips:

Start by trying to list up to 3 things you are grateful for each day in the blanks provided

To appreciate where you are now, it can help to reflect on the hard times you've already overcome

Share your gratitude with others. Be sure to let someone know you appreciate them

Daily Gratitude

Today I am thankful for: (list 3 things)

_____

_____

_____

What would make today great?

_____

_____

_____

I am proud of myself today for:

_____

I am looking forward to:

_____

My main focus for today:

_____

Date _____

Daily Gratitude

Today I am thankful for: (list 3 things)

_____

_____

_____

What would make today great?

_____

_____

_____

I am proud of myself today for:

_____

I am looking forward to:

_____

My main focus for today:

_____

Date _____

Daily Gratitude

Today I am thankful for: (list 3 things)

_____

_____

_____

What would make today great?

_____

_____

_____

I am proud of myself today for:

_____

I am looking forward to:

_____

My main focus for today:

_____

Date _____

Daily Gratitude

Today I am thankful for: (list 3 things)

_____

_____

_____

What would make today great?

_____

_____

_____

I am proud of myself today for:

_____

I am looking forward to:

_____

My main focus for today:

_____

Date _____

Daily Gratitude

Today I am thankful for: (list 3 things)

_____

_____

_____

What would make today great?

_____

_____

_____

I am proud of myself today for:

_____

I am looking forward to:

_____

My main focus for today:

_____

Date _____

Daily Gratitude

Today I am thankful for: (list 3 things)

_____

_____

_____

What would make today great?

_____

_____

_____

I am proud of myself today for:

_____

I am looking forward to:

_____

My main focus for today:

_____

Date _____

Daily Gratitude

Today I am thankful for: (list 3 things)

_____

_____

_____

What would make today great?

_____

_____

_____

I am proud of myself today for:

_____

I am looking forward to:

_____

My main focus for today:

_____

Date _____

Daily Gratitude

Today I am thankful for: (list 3 things)

_____

_____

_____

What would make today great?

_____

_____

_____

I am proud of myself today for:

_____

I am looking forward to:

_____

My main focus for today:

_____

Date _____

Daily Gratitude

Today I am thankful for: (list 3 things)

_____

_____

_____

What would make today great?

_____

_____

_____

I am proud of myself today for:

_____

I am looking forward to:

_____

My main focus for today:

_____

Date _____

Daily Gratitude

Today I am thankful for: (list 3 things)

_____

_____

_____

What would make today great?

_____

_____

_____

I am proud of myself today for:

_____

I am looking forward to:

_____

My main focus for today:

_____

Date _____

Daily Gratitude

Today I am thankful for: (list 3 things)

_____

_____

_____

What would make today great?

_____

_____

_____

I am proud of myself today for:

_____

I am looking forward to:

_____

My main focus for today:

_____

Date _____

Daily Gratitude

Today I am thankful for: (list 3 things)

_____

_____

_____

What would make today great?

_____

_____

_____

I am proud of myself today for:

_____

I am looking forward to:

_____

My main focus for today:

_____

Date _____

Daily Gratitude

Today I am thankful for: (list 3 things)

_____

_____

_____

What would make today great?

_____

_____

_____

I am proud of myself today for:

_____

I am looking forward to:

_____

My main focus for today:

_____

Date _____

Daily Gratitude

Today I am thankful for: (list 3 things)

_____

_____

_____

What would make today great?

_____

_____

_____

I am proud of myself today for:

_____

I am looking forward to:

_____

My main focus for today:

_____

Date _____

Daily Gratitude

Today I am thankful for: (list 3 things)

_____

_____

_____

What would make today great?

_____

_____

_____

I am proud of myself today for:

_____

I am looking forward to:

_____

My main focus for today:

_____

Date _____

Daily Gratitude

Today I am thankful for: (list 3 things)

_____

_____

_____

What would make today great?

_____

_____

_____

I am proud of myself today for:

_____

I am looking forward to:

_____

My main focus for today:

_____

Date _____

Daily Gratitude

Today I am thankful for: (list 3 things)

_____

_____

_____

What would make today great?

_____

_____

_____

I am proud of myself today for:

_____

I am looking forward to:

_____

My main focus for today:

_____

Date _____

Daily Gratitude

Today I am thankful for: (list 3 things)

_____

_____

_____

What would make today great?

_____

_____

_____

I am proud of myself today for:

_____

I am looking forward to:

_____

My main focus for today:

_____

Date _____

Daily Gratitude

Today I am thankful for: (list 3 things)

_____

_____

_____

What would make today great?

_____

_____

_____

I am proud of myself today for:

_____

I am looking forward to:

_____

My main focus for today:

_____

Date _____

Daily Gratitude

Today I am thankful for: (list 3 things)

_____

_____

_____

What would make today great?

_____

_____

_____

I am proud of myself today for:

_____

I am looking forward to:

_____

My main focus for today:

_____

Date _____

Daily Gratitude

Today I am thankful for: (list 3 things)

_____

_____

_____

What would make today great?

_____

_____

_____

I am proud of myself today for:

_____

I am looking forward to:

_____

My main focus for today:

_____

Date _____

Daily Gratitude

Today I am thankful for: (list 3 things)

_____

_____

_____

What would make today great?

_____

_____

_____

I am proud of myself today for:

_____

I am looking forward to:

_____

My main focus for today:

_____

Date _____

Daily Gratitude

Today I am thankful for: (list 3 things)

_____

_____

_____

What would make today great?

_____

_____

_____

I am proud of myself today for:

_____

I am looking forward to:

_____

My main focus for today:

_____

Date _____

Daily Gratitude

Today I am thankful for: (list 3 things)

_____

_____

_____

What would make today great?

_____

_____

_____

I am proud of myself today for:

_____

I am looking forward to:

_____

My main focus for today:

_____

Date _____

Daily Gratitude

Today I am thankful for: (list 3 things)

_____

_____

_____

What would make today great?

_____

_____

_____

I am proud of myself today for:

_____

I am looking forward to:

_____

My main focus for today:

_____

Date _____

Daily Gratitude

Today I am thankful for: (list 3 things)

_____

_____

_____

What would make today great?

_____

_____

_____

I am proud of myself today for:

_____

I am looking forward to:

_____

My main focus for today:

_____

Date _____

Daily Gratitude

Today I am thankful for: (list 3 things)

_____

_____

_____

What would make today great?

_____

_____

_____

I am proud of myself today for:

_____

I am looking forward to:

_____

My main focus for today:

_____

Date _____

Daily Gratitude

Today I am thankful for: (list 3 things)

_____

_____

_____

What would make today great?

_____

_____

_____

I am proud of myself today for:

_____

I am looking forward to:

_____

My main focus for today:

_____

Date _____

Daily Gratitude

Today I am thankful for: (list 3 things)

_____

_____

_____

What would make today great?

_____

_____

_____

I am proud of myself today for:

_____

I am looking forward to:

_____

My main focus for today:

_____

Date _____

Daily Gratitude

Today I am thankful for: (list 3 things)

_____

_____

_____

What would make today great?

_____

_____

_____

I am proud of myself today for:

_____

I am looking forward to:

_____

My main focus for today:

_____

Date _____

Daily Gratitude

Today I am thankful for: (list 3 things)

_____

_____

_____

What would make today great?

_____

_____

_____

I am proud of myself today for:

_____

I am looking forward to:

_____

My main focus for today:

_____

Date _____

Daily Gratitude

Today I am thankful for: (list 3 things)

_____

_____

_____

What would make today great?

_____

_____

_____

I am proud of myself today for:

_____

I am looking forward to:

_____

My main focus for today:

_____

Date _____

Daily Gratitude

Today I am thankful for: (list 3 things)

_____

_____

_____

What would make today great?

_____

_____

_____

I am proud of myself today for:

_____

I am looking forward to:

_____

My main focus for today:

_____

Date _____

Daily Gratitude

Today I am thankful for: (list 3 things)

_____

_____

_____

What would make today great?

_____

_____

_____

I am proud of myself today for:

_____

I am looking forward to:

_____

My main focus for today:

_____

Date _____

Daily Gratitude

Today I am thankful for: (list 3 things)

_____

_____

_____

What would make today great?

_____

_____

_____

I am proud of myself today for:

_____

I am looking forward to:

_____

My main focus for today:

_____

Date _____

Daily Gratitude

Today I am thankful for: (list 3 things)

_____

_____

_____

What would make today great?

_____

_____

_____

I am proud of myself today for:

_____

I am looking forward to:

_____

My main focus for today:

_____

Date _____

Daily Gratitude

Today I am thankful for: (list 3 things)

_____

_____

_____

What would make today great?

_____

_____

_____

I am proud of myself today for:

_____

I am looking forward to:

_____

My main focus for today:

_____

Date _____

Daily Gratitude

Today I am thankful for: (list 3 things)

_____

_____

_____

What would make today great?

_____

_____

_____

I am proud of myself today for:

_____

I am looking forward to:

_____

My main focus for today:

_____

Date _____

Daily Gratitude

Today I am thankful for: (list 3 things)

_____

_____

_____

What would make today great?

_____

_____

_____

I am proud of myself today for:

_____

I am looking forward to:

_____

My main focus for today:

_____

Date _____

Daily Gratitude

Today I am thankful for: (list 3 things)

_____

_____

_____

What would make today great?

_____

_____

_____

I am proud of myself today for:

_____

I am looking forward to:

_____

My main focus for today:

_____

Date _____

Daily Gratitude

Today I am thankful for: (list 3 things)

_____

_____

_____

What would make today great?

_____

_____

_____

I am proud of myself today for:

_____

I am looking forward to:

_____

My main focus for today:

_____

Date _____

Daily Gratitude

Today I am thankful for: (list 3 things)

_____

_____

_____

What would make today great?

_____

_____

_____

I am proud of myself today for:

_____

I am looking forward to:

_____

My main focus for today:

_____

Date _____

Daily Gratitude

Today I am thankful for: (list 3 things)

_____

_____

_____

What would make today great?

_____

_____

_____

I am proud of myself today for:

_____

I am looking forward to:

_____

My main focus for today:

_____

Date _____

Daily Gratitude

Today I am thankful for: (list 3 things)

_____

_____

_____

What would make today great?

_____

_____

_____

I am proud of myself today for:

_____

I am looking forward to:

_____

My main focus for today:

_____

Date _____

Daily Gratitude

Today I am thankful for: (list 3 things)

_____

_____

_____

What would make today great?

_____

_____

_____

I am proud of myself today for:

_____

I am looking forward to:

_____

My main focus for today:

_____

Date _____

Daily Gratitude

Today I am thankful for: (list 3 things)

_____

_____

_____

What would make today great?

_____

_____

_____

I am proud of myself today for:

_____

I am looking forward to:

_____

My main focus for today:

_____

Date _____

Daily Gratitude

Today I am thankful for: (list 3 things)

_____

_____

_____

What would make today great?

_____

_____

_____

I am proud of myself today for:

_____

I am looking forward to:

_____

My main focus for today:

_____

Date _____

Daily Gratitude

Today I am thankful for: (list 3 things)

_____

_____

_____

What would make today great?

_____

_____

_____

I am proud of myself today for:

_____

I am looking forward to:

_____

My main focus for today:

_____

Date _____

Daily Gratitude

Today I am thankful for: (list 3 things)

_____

_____

_____

What would make today great?

_____

_____

_____

I am proud of myself today for:

_____

I am looking forward to:

_____

My main focus for today:

_____

Date _____

Daily Gratitude

Today I am thankful for: (list 3 things)

_____

_____

_____

What would make today great?

_____

_____

_____

I am proud of myself today for:

_____

I am looking forward to:

_____

My main focus for today:

_____

Date _____

Daily Gratitude

Today I am thankful for: (list 3 things)

_____

_____

_____

What would make today great?

_____

_____

_____

I am proud of myself today for:

_____

I am looking forward to:

_____

My main focus for today:

_____

Date _____

Daily Gratitude

Today I am thankful for: (list 3 things)

_____

_____

_____

What would make today great?

_____

_____

_____

I am proud of myself today for:

_____

I am looking forward to:

_____

My main focus for today:

_____

Date _____

Daily Gratitude

Today I am thankful for: (list 3 things)

_____

_____

_____

What would make today great?

_____

_____

_____

I am proud of myself today for:

_____

I am looking forward to:

_____

My main focus for today:

_____

Date _____

Daily Gratitude

Today I am thankful for: (list 3 things)

_____

_____

_____

What would make today great?

_____

_____

_____

I am proud of myself today for:

_____

I am looking forward to:

_____

My main focus for today:

_____

Date _____

Daily Gratitude

Today I am thankful for: (list 3 things)

_____

_____

_____

What would make today great?

_____

_____

_____

I am proud of myself today for:

_____

I am looking forward to:

_____

My main focus for today:

_____

Date _____

Daily Gratitude

Today I am thankful for: (list 3 things)

_____

_____

_____

What would make today great?

_____

_____

_____

I am proud of myself today for:

_____

I am looking forward to:

_____

My main focus for today:

_____

Date _____

Daily Gratitude

Today I am thankful for: (list 3 things)

_____

_____

_____

What would make today great?

_____

_____

_____

I am proud of myself today for:

_____

I am looking forward to:

_____

My main focus for today:

_____

Date _____

Daily Gratitude

Today I am thankful for: (list 3 things)

_____

_____

_____

What would make today great?

_____

_____

_____

I am proud of myself today for:

_____

I am looking forward to:

_____

My main focus for today:

_____

Date _____

Daily Gratitude

Today I am thankful for: (list 3 things)

_____

_____

_____

What would make today great?

_____

_____

_____

I am proud of myself today for:

_____

I am looking forward to:

_____

My main focus for today:

_____

Date _____

Daily Gratitude

Today I am thankful for: (list 3 things)

_____

_____

_____

What would make today great?

_____

_____

_____

I am proud of myself today for:

_____

I am looking forward to:

_____

My main focus for today:

_____

Date _____

Daily Gratitude

Today I am thankful for: (list 3 things)

_____

_____

_____

What would make today great?

_____

_____

_____

I am proud of myself today for:

_____

I am looking forward to:

_____

My main focus for today:

_____

Date _____

Daily Gratitude

Today I am thankful for: (list 3 things)

_____

_____

_____

What would make today great?

_____

_____

_____

I am proud of myself today for:

_____

I am looking forward to:

_____

My main focus for today:

_____

Date _____

Daily Gratitude

Today I am thankful for: (list 3 things)

_____

_____

_____

What would make today great?

_____

_____

_____

I am proud of myself today for:

_____

I am looking forward to:

_____

My main focus for today:

_____

Date _____

Daily Gratitude

Today I am thankful for: (list 3 things)

_____

_____

_____

What would make today great?

_____

_____

_____

I am proud of myself today for:

_____

I am looking forward to:

_____

My main focus for today:

_____

Date _____

Daily Gratitude

Today I am thankful for: (list 3 things)

_____

_____

_____

What would make today great?

_____

_____

_____

I am proud of myself today for:

_____

I am looking forward to:

_____

My main focus for today:

_____

Date _____

Daily Gratitude

Today I am thankful for: (list 3 things)

_____

_____

_____

What would make today great?

_____

_____

_____

I am proud of myself today for:

_____

I am looking forward to:

_____

My main focus for today:

_____

Date _____

Daily Gratitude

Today I am thankful for: (list 3 things)

_____

_____

_____

What would make today great?

_____

_____

_____

I am proud of myself today for:

_____

I am looking forward to:

_____

My main focus for today:

_____

Date _____

Daily Gratitude

Today I am thankful for: (list 3 things)

_____

_____

_____

What would make today great?

_____

_____

_____

I am proud of myself today for:

_____

I am looking forward to:

_____

My main focus for today:

_____

Date _____

Daily Gratitude

Today I am thankful for: (list 3 things)

_____

_____

_____

What would make today great?

_____

_____

_____

I am proud of myself today for:

_____

I am looking forward to:

_____

My main focus for today:

_____

Date _____

Daily Gratitude

Today I am thankful for: (list 3 things)

_____

_____

_____

What would make today great?

_____

_____

_____

I am proud of myself today for:

_____

I am looking forward to:

_____

My main focus for today:

_____

Date _____

Daily Gratitude

Today I am thankful for: (list 3 things)

_____

_____

_____

What would make today great?

_____

_____

_____

I am proud of myself today for:

_____

I am looking forward to:

_____

My main focus for today:

_____

Date _____

Daily Gratitude

Today I am thankful for: (list 3 things)

_____

_____

_____

What would make today great?

_____

_____

_____

I am proud of myself today for:

_____

I am looking forward to:

_____

My main focus for today:

_____

Date _____

Daily Gratitude

Today I am thankful for: (list 3 things)

_____

_____

_____

What would make today great?

_____

_____

_____

I am proud of myself today for:

_____

I am looking forward to:

_____

My main focus for today:

_____

Date _____

Daily Gratitude

Today I am thankful for: (list 3 things)

_____

_____

_____

What would make today great?

_____

_____

_____

I am proud of myself today for:

_____

I am looking forward to:

_____

My main focus for today:

_____

Date _____

Daily Gratitude

Today I am thankful for: (list 3 things)

_____

_____

_____

What would make today great?

_____

_____

_____

I am proud of myself today for:

_____

I am looking forward to:

_____

My main focus for today:

_____

Date _____

Daily Gratitude

Today I am thankful for: (list 3 things)

_____

_____

_____

What would make today great?

_____

_____

_____

I am proud of myself today for:

_____

I am looking forward to:

_____

My main focus for today:

_____

Date _____

Daily Gratitude

Today I am thankful for: (list 3 things)

_____

_____

_____

What would make today great?

_____

_____

_____

I am proud of myself today for:

_____

I am looking forward to:

_____

My main focus for today:

_____

Date _____

Daily Gratitude

Today I am thankful for: (list 3 things)

_____

_____

_____

What would make today great?

_____

_____

_____

I am proud of myself today for:

_____

I am looking forward to:

_____

My main focus for today:

_____

Date _____

Daily Gratitude

Today I am thankful for: (list 3 things)

_____

_____

_____

What would make today great?

_____

_____

_____

I am proud of myself today for:

_____

I am looking forward to:

_____

My main focus for today:

_____

Date _____

Daily Gratitude

Today I am thankful for: (list 3 things)

_____

_____

_____

What would make today great?

_____

_____

I am proud of myself today for:

_____

I am looking forward to:

_____

My main focus for today:

_____

Date _____

Daily Gratitude

Today I am thankful for: (list 3 things)

_____

_____

_____

What would make today great?

_____

_____

_____

I am proud of myself today for:

_____

I am looking forward to:

_____

My main focus for today:

_____

Date _____

Daily Gratitude

Today I am thankful for: (list 3 things)

_____

_____

_____

What would make today great?

_____

_____

_____

I am proud of myself today for:

_____

I am looking forward to:

_____

My main focus for today:

_____

Date _____

Daily Gratitude

Today I am thankful for: (list 3 things)

_____

_____

_____

What would make today great?

_____

_____

_____

I am proud of myself today for:

_____

I am looking forward to:

_____

My main focus for today:

_____

Date _____

Daily Gratitude

Today I am thankful for: (list 3 things)

_____

_____

_____

What would make today great?

_____

_____

_____

I am proud of myself today for:

_____

I am looking forward to:

_____

My main focus for today:

_____

Date _____

Daily Gratitude

Today I am thankful for: (list 3 things)

_____

_____

_____

What would make today great?

_____

_____

_____

I am proud of myself today for:

_____

I am looking forward to:

_____

My main focus for today:

_____

Date _____

Daily Gratitude

Today I am thankful for: (list 3 things)

_____

_____

_____

What would make today great?

_____

_____

_____

I am proud of myself today for:

_____

I am looking forward to:

_____

My main focus for today:

_____

Date _____

Daily Gratitude

Today I am thankful for: (list 3 things)

_____

_____

_____

What would make today great?

_____

_____

_____

I am proud of myself today for:

_____

I am looking forward to:

_____

My main focus for today:

_____

Date _____

Daily Gratitude

Today I am thankful for: (list 3 things)

_____

_____

_____

What would make today great?

_____

_____

_____

I am proud of myself today for:

_____

I am looking forward to:

_____

My main focus for today:

_____

Date _____

Daily Gratitude

Today I am thankful for: (list 3 things)

_____

_____

_____

What would make today great?

_____

_____

_____

I am proud of myself today for:

_____

I am looking forward to:

_____

My main focus for today:

_____

Date _____

Daily Gratitude

Today I am thankful for: (list 3 things)

_____

_____

_____

What would make today great?

_____

_____

_____

I am proud of myself today for:

_____

I am looking forward to:

_____

My main focus for today:

_____

Date _____

Daily Gratitude

Today I am thankful for: (list 3 things)

_____

_____

_____

What would make today great?

_____

_____

_____

I am proud of myself today for:

_____

I am looking forward to:

_____

My main focus for today:

_____

Date _____

Daily Gratitude

Today I am thankful for: (list 3 things)

_____

_____

_____

What would make today great?

_____

_____

_____

I am proud of myself today for:

_____

I am looking forward to:

_____

My main focus for today:

_____

Date _____

Daily Gratitude

Today I am thankful for: (list 3 things)

_____

_____

_____

What would make today great?

_____

_____

_____

I am proud of myself today for:

_____

I am looking forward to:

_____

My main focus for today:

_____

Date _____

Daily Gratitude

Today I am thankful for: (list 3 things)

_____

_____

_____

What would make today great?

_____

_____

_____

I am proud of myself today for:

_____

I am looking forward to:

_____

My main focus for today:

_____

Date _____

Daily Gratitude

Today I am thankful for: (list 3 things)

_____

_____

_____

What would make today great?

_____

_____

_____

I am proud of myself today for:

_____

I am looking forward to:

_____

My main focus for today:

_____

Date _____

Daily Gratitude

Today I am thankful for: (list 3 things)

_____

_____

_____

What would make today great?

_____

_____

_____

I am proud of myself today for:

_____

I am looking forward to:

_____

My main focus for today:

_____

Date _____

Daily Gratitude

Today I am thankful for: (list 3 things)

_____

_____

_____

What would make today great?

_____

_____

_____

I am proud of myself today for:

_____

I am looking forward to:

_____

My main focus for today:

_____

Date _____

Daily Gratitude

Today I am thankful for: (list 3 things)

_____

_____

_____

What would make today great?

_____

_____

_____

I am proud of myself today for:

_____

I am looking forward to:

_____

My main focus for today:

_____

Date _____

Daily Gratitude

Today I am thankful for: (list 3 things)

_____

_____

_____

What would make today great?

_____

_____

_____

I am proud of myself today for:

_____

I am looking forward to:

_____

My main focus for today:

_____

Date _____

Daily Gratitude

Today I am thankful for: (list 3 things)

_____

_____

_____

What would make today great?

_____

_____

_____

I am proud of myself today for:

_____

I am looking forward to:

_____

My main focus for today:

_____

Date _____

Daily Gratitude

Today I am thankful for: (list 3 things)

_____

_____

_____

What would make today great?

_____

_____

_____

I am proud of myself today for:

_____

I am looking forward to:

_____

My main focus for today:

_____

Date _____

Daily Gratitude

Today I am thankful for: (list 3 things)

_____

_____

_____

What would make today great?

_____

_____

_____

I am proud of myself today for:

_____

I am looking forward to:

_____

My main focus for today:

_____

Date _____

Daily Gratitude

Today I am thankful for: (list 3 things)

_____

_____

_____

What would make today great?

_____

_____

_____

I am proud of myself today for:

_____

I am looking forward to:

_____

My main focus for today:

_____

Date _____

Daily Gratitude

Today I am thankful for: (list 3 things)

_____

_____

_____

What would make today great?

_____

_____

_____

I am proud of myself today for:

_____

I am looking forward to:

_____

My main focus for today:

_____

Date _____

Daily Gratitude

Today I am thankful for: (list 3 things)

_____

_____

_____

What would make today great?

_____

_____

_____

I am proud of myself today for:

_____

I am looking forward to:

_____

My main focus for today:

_____

Date _____

Daily Gratitude

Today I am thankful for: (list 3 things)

_____

_____

_____

What would make today great?

_____

_____

_____

I am proud of myself today for:

_____

I am looking forward to:

_____

My main focus for today:

_____

Date _____

Daily Gratitude

Today I am thankful for: (list 3 things)

_____

_____

_____

What would make today great?

_____

_____

_____

I am proud of myself today for:

_____

I am looking forward to:

_____

My main focus for today:

_____

Date _____

Daily Gratitude

Today I am thankful for: (list 3 things)

_____

_____

_____

What would make today great?

_____

_____

_____

I am proud of myself today for:

_____

I am looking forward to:

_____

My main focus for today:

_____

Date _____

Daily Gratitude

Today I am thankful for: (list 3 things)

_____

_____

_____

What would make today great?

_____

_____

_____

I am proud of myself today for:

_____

I am looking forward to:

_____

My main focus for today:

_____

Date _____

Daily Gratitude

Today I am thankful for: (list 3 things)

_____

_____

_____

What would make today great?

_____

_____

_____

I am proud of myself today for:

_____

I am looking forward to:

_____

My main focus for today:

_____

Date _____

Daily Gratitude

Today I am thankful for: (list 3 things)

_____

_____

_____

What would make today great?

_____

_____

_____

I am proud of myself today for:

_____

I am looking forward to:

_____

My main focus for today:

_____

Date _____

Daily Gratitude

Today I am thankful for: (list 3 things)

_____

_____

_____

What would make today great?

_____

_____

_____

I am proud of myself today for:

_____

I am looking forward to:

_____

My main focus for today:

_____

Date _____

Daily Gratitude

Today I am thankful for: (list 3 things)

_____

_____

_____

What would make today great?

_____

_____

_____

I am proud of myself today for:

_____

I am looking forward to:

_____

My main focus for today:

_____

Date _____

Daily Gratitude

Today I am thankful for: (list 3 things)

_____

_____

_____

What would make today great?

_____

_____

_____

I am proud of myself today for:

_____

I am looking forward to:

_____

My main focus for today:

_____

Date _____

Daily Gratitude

Today I am thankful for: (list 3 things)

_____

_____

_____

What would make today great?

_____

_____

_____

I am proud of myself today for:

_____

I am looking forward to:

_____

My main focus for today:

_____

Date _____

Daily Gratitude

Today I am thankful for: (list 3 things)

_____

_____

_____

What would make today great?

_____

_____

_____

I am proud of myself today for:

_____

I am looking forward to:

_____

My main focus for today:

_____

Date _____

Daily Gratitude

Today I am thankful for: (list 3 things)

_____

_____

_____

What would make today great?

_____

_____

_____

I am proud of myself today for:

_____

I am looking forward to:

_____

My main focus for today:

_____

Date _____

Made in the USA
Las Vegas, NV
31 October 2023